D1005646

YOU'RE
NEVER
TOO *old*
to...

LIZZIE
CORNWALL

summersdale

YOU'RE NEVER TOO OLD TO...

An Hachette UK Company
www.hachette.co.uk

Summersdale Publishers Ltd
Part of Octopus Publishing Group Limited
Carmelite House
50 Victoria Embankment
LONDON
EC4Y 0DZ
UK

www.summersdale.com

Printed and bound in China

ISBN: 978-1-78783-244-2

Substantial discounts on bulk quantities of Summersdale books are available to corporations, professional associations and other organizations. For details contact general enquiries: telephone: +44 (0) 1243 771107 or email: enquiries@summersdale.com.

TO.............................

FROM..........................

YOU'RE NEVER
TOO OLD TO...

YOU'RE NEVER
TOO OLD TO...

... LICK ALL THE CHOCOLATE
OFF YOUR COOKIE FIRST.

YOU'RE NEVER
TOO OLD TO...

... FALL IN LOVE.

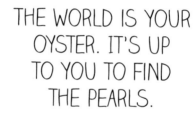

YOU'RE NEVER
TOO OLD TO...

... WRITE LETTERS TO YOUR
HEROES TELLING THEM WHY
YOU ADMIRE THEM.

YOU'RE NEVER
TOO OLD TO...

... FEED THE DUCKS.

YOU'RE NEVER
TOO OLD TO...

... WEAR SEQUINS.

YOU'RE NEVER
TOO OLD TO...

... DANCE ALL NIGHT –
OR AT LEAST UNTIL THE
NEIGHBOURS START
TO COMPLAIN!

LIFE IS BEING ON THE
WIRE, EVERYTHING ELSE
IS JUST WAITING.

Karl Wallenda

YOU'RE NEVER
TOO OLD TO...

... BREAK THE INTERNET.

YOU'RE NEVER
TOO OLD TO...

... BEGIN WITH DESSERT.

THE QUESTION ISN'T WHO
IS GOING TO LET ME;
IT'S WHO IS GOING
TO STOP ME.

Ayn Rand

YOU'RE NEVER
TOO OLD TO...

... TRY A NEW SPORT,
LIKE SKY-DIVING.

YOU'RE NEVER
TOO OLD TO...

... GIVE AN UNEXPECTED
PRESENT TO A FRIEND.

YOU'RE NEVER
TOO OLD TO...

... BE CALLED "YOUNG
MAN" OR "YOUNG LADY"
BY SOMEBODY.

YOU'RE NEVER
TOO OLD TO...

... LEARN SOMETHING SILLY,
LIKE BACKWARDS WRITING.

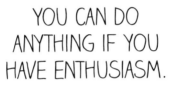

YOU CAN DO
ANYTHING IF YOU
HAVE ENTHUSIASM.

Henry Ford

YOU'RE NEVER
TOO OLD TO...

... TRY A NEW TYPE
OF CHEESE.

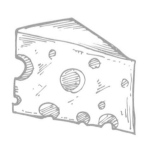

YOU'RE NEVER
TOO OLD TO...

... TICKLE A
DOG'S BELLY.

THE UNIVERSE HAS NO RESTRICTIONS. YOU PLACE RESTRICTIONS ON THE UNIVERSE WITH YOUR EXPECTATIONS.

Deepak Chopra

YOU'RE NEVER TOO OLD TO...

... DO A STRIPTEASE!

YOU'RE NEVER
TOO OLD TO...

... GO TO SEE
THE PENGUINS
AT THE ZOO.

YOU'RE NEVER
TOO OLD TO...

... ACT LIKE
A TEENAGER.

YOU'RE NEVER TOO OLD TO...

... BE CONFUSED.

ONLY THOSE WHO WILL
RISK GOING TOO FAR CAN
POSSIBLY FIND OUT HOW
FAR ONE CAN GO.

T. S. Eliot

YOU'RE NEVER
TOO OLD TO...

... GO STARGAZING.

YOU'RE NEVER
TOO OLD TO...

... EAT ANOTHER PIECE
OF CAKE.

THE BEST IS
YET TO BE.

Robert Browning

YOU'RE NEVER
TOO OLD TO...

... DANCE
THE TANGO.

YOU'RE NEVER
TOO OLD TO...

... PREFER DIAMONDS.

YOU'RE NEVER
TOO OLD TO...

... TAKE UP YOGA.

IT ALWAYS SEEMS
IMPOSSIBLE UNTIL
IT'S DONE.

Anonymous

YOU'RE NEVER
TOO OLD TO...

... GO INSIDE THE
GREAT PYRAMID.

YOU'RE NEVER
TOO OLD TO...

... THROW A PARTY.

IT IS NEVER TOO LATE
TO BE WHAT YOU
MIGHT HAVE BEEN.

Adelaide Anne Procter

YOU'RE NEVER
TOO OLD TO...

... WRITE A BESTSELLER.

YOU'RE NEVER
TOO OLD TO...

... DO SOMETHING
DARING.

YOU'RE NEVER
TOO OLD TO...

... WEAR PATTERNED SOCKS.

YOU'RE NEVER
TOO OLD TO...

... PLANT A TREE
AND DEDICATE IT
TO SOMEONE.

THE BEST TIME TO
PLANT A TREE WAS
TWENTY YEARS AGO.
THE SECOND BEST
TIME IS NOW.

Chinese proverb

YOU'RE NEVER
TOO OLD TO...

... RIDE A TANDEM.

YOU'RE NEVER
TOO OLD TO...

... MAKE SILLY FACES AT
PEOPLE WHEN THEY'RE
NOT LOOKING.

FOREVER IS
COMPOSED
OF NOWS.

Emily Dickinson

YOU'RE NEVER
TOO OLD TO...

... LIE UNDER A BIG TREE
AND SPEND AN HOUR
JUST GAZING UP AT
THE BRANCHES.

YOU'RE NEVER
TOO OLD TO...

... CONSIDER ROLLER
SKATES AS A MODE
OF TRANSPORT.

YOU'RE NEVER
TOO OLD TO...

... WATCH THE WAVES
ROLLING IN TO SHORE.

YOU'RE NEVER
TOO OLD TO...

... TOUCH AN ICEBERG.

MAY YOU LIVE ALL THE
DAYS OF YOUR LIFE.

Jonathan Swift

YOU'RE NEVER
TOO OLD TO...

... JUMP OVER THE
CRACKS IN THE PAVEMENT.

YOU'RE NEVER
TOO OLD TO...

... GIVE SOMEONE
FLOWERS.

LIGHT TOMORROW
WITH TODAY.

*Elizabeth Barrett
Browning*

YOU'RE NEVER
TOO OLD TO...

... GET ON THE NEXT TRAIN
OUT OF TOWN AND GET
OFF SOMEWHERE NEW.

YOU'RE NEVER
TOO OLD TO...

... LAUGH. THINK ABOUT
SOMETHING THAT MADE
YOU LAUGH AND GIGGLE
ALL OVER AGAIN.

YOU'RE NEVER
TOO OLD TO...

... WIN THE LOTTERY.
HOW WOULD YOU
SPEND IT?

YOU'RE NEVER
TOO OLD TO...

... SPEND AN
ENTIRE SUMMER
DAY BAREFOOT.

BE PRESENT IN ALL
THINGS AND THANKFUL
FOR ALL THINGS.

Maya Angelou

YOU'RE NEVER
TOO OLD TO...

... COUNT
YOUR BLESSINGS.

YOU'RE NEVER
TOO OLD TO...

... TAKE UP FENCING.

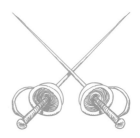

YOU ARE NEVER TOO
OLD TO SET ANOTHER
GOAL OR TO DREAM
A NEW DREAM.

Les Brown

YOU'RE NEVER
TOO OLD TO...

... GO UP
IN A HOT-AIR
BALLOON.

YOU'RE NEVER
TOO OLD TO...

... DYE YOUR HAIR PINK
AND GET A TATTOO.

YOU'RE NEVER
TOO OLD TO...

... BE A FASHIONISTA.

YOU'RE NEVER
TOO OLD TO...

... TRAVEL FIRST CLASS
AND TREAT YOURSELF
TO LUNCH IN
THE DINING CAR.

ALL LIFE IS AN EXPERIMENT. THE MORE EXPERIMENTS YOU MAKE THE BETTER.

Ralph Waldo Emerson

YOU'RE NEVER
TOO OLD TO...

... DESIGN A SPACE ROCKET.

YOU'RE NEVER
TOO OLD TO...

... WORK IN A HOMELESS
SHELTER FOR A DAY.

LIVE THE ACTUAL MOMENT.
ONLY THIS MOMENT IS LIFE.

Thich Nhât Hạnh

YOU'RE NEVER
TOO OLD TO...

... WALK DOWN THE STREET,
BOPPING YOUR HEAD TO
THE LATEST TUNES.

YOU'RE NEVER TOO OLD TO...

... WEAR HIGH HEELS.

YOU'RE NEVER
TOO OLD TO...

... EAT AN
ICE CREAM
SUNDAE.

YOU'RE NEVER
TOO OLD TO...

... SHARE A
PRIVATE JOKE.

THE SOUL'S JOY
LIES IN DOING.

Percy Bysshe Shelley

YOU'RE NEVER
TOO OLD TO...

... HAVE A CRUSH ON
A MOVIE STAR.

YOU'RE NEVER
TOO OLD TO...

... LEARN TO MEDITATE.

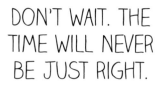

DON'T WAIT. THE
TIME WILL NEVER
BE JUST RIGHT.

Napoleon Hill

YOU'RE NEVER
TOO OLD TO...

... CLIMB TO THE TOP
OF A TOWER AND
ADMIRE THE VIEW.

YOU'RE NEVER
TOO OLD TO...

... GO SKINNY-DIPPING.

YOU'RE NEVER
TOO OLD TO...

... STAY IN THE
HONEYMOON
SUITE OF YOUR
FAVOURITE HOTEL.

YOU'RE NEVER
TOO OLD TO...

... WRITE A POEM.

LIFE SHRINKS OR
EXPANDS ACCORDING
TO ONE'S COURAGE.

Anaïs Nin

YOU'RE NEVER
TOO OLD TO...

... BE WHISKED OFF
YOUR FEET.

YOU'RE NEVER
TOO OLD TO...

... BECOME A
WINE BUFF.

YOU CAN DO
ANYTHING YOU SET
YOUR MIND TO.

Benjamin Franklin

YOU'RE NEVER
TOO OLD TO...

... SIT ON
SANTA'S KNEE.

YOU'RE NEVER
TOO OLD TO...

... GO WILD AT
A ROCK FESTIVAL.

YOU'RE NEVER
TOO OLD TO...

... LEARN A NEW LANGUAGE.

YOU'RE NEVER
TOO OLD TO...

... TRY SUSHI FOR
THE FIRST TIME.

IT IS EITHER EASY
OR IMPOSSIBLE.

Salvador Dalí

YOU'RE NEVER
TOO OLD TO...

... WEAR A FLOWER
IN YOUR HAIR.

YOU'RE NEVER
TOO OLD TO...

... DISCOVER THAT
YOU ACTUALLY *DO*
LIKE HOT SAUCE.

YOU'RE NEVER
TOO OLD TO...

... GO BLONDE.

... DRINK A MILKSHAKE
THROUGH A STRAW AND
MAKE LOUD BUBBLING
SOUNDS WHEN YOU
GET TO THE BOTTOM
OF THE GLASS.

EVERY GREAT DREAM
BEGINS WITH
A DREAMER.

Anonymous

YOU'RE NEVER
TOO OLD TO...

... OFFER
TO HELP
SOMEONE.

YOU'RE NEVER
TOO OLD TO...

... BUILD A SANDCASTLE.

LIFE IS A GREAT BIG
CANVAS, AND YOU SHOULD
THROW ALL THE PAINT ON
IT YOU CAN.

Danny Kaye

YOU'RE NEVER
TOO OLD TO...

... GET INTO A NEW
STYLE OF MUSIC.

YOU'RE NEVER
TOO OLD TO...

... RUN THAT RACE.

YOU'RE NEVER
TOO OLD TO...

... MAKE SOMEONE'S DAY.

YOU'RE NEVER
TOO OLD TO...

... BE MISCHIEVOUS.

IF YOU DON'T GO,
YOU'LL NEVER KNOW.

Robert de Niro

YOU'RE NEVER
TOO OLD TO...

... WATCH THE
SUN RISE.

YOU'RE NEVER
TOO OLD TO...

... DO A
SILLY WALK.

LET YOUR JOY BE IN
YOUR JOURNEY – NOT
IN SOME DISTANT GOAL.

Tim Cook

YOU'RE NEVER
TOO OLD TO...

... GET IN TOUCH WITH
AN OLD FRIEND.

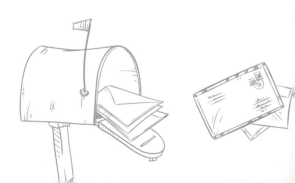

YOU'RE NEVER
TOO OLD TO...

... SEND A VALENTINE'S
CARD.

YOU'RE NEVER
TOO OLD TO...

... PLACE A BET.

YOU'RE NEVER
TOO OLD TO...

... EAT SOMETHING
NAUGHTY BUT NICE.

THROW CAUTION
TO THE WIND AND
JUST DO IT.

Carrie Underwood

YOU'RE NEVER
TOO OLD TO...

... KISS SOMEONE FOR
THE FIRST TIME.

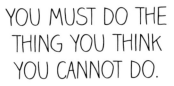

YOU'RE NEVER
TOO OLD TO...

... JUMP DOWN
THE LAST STEP.

YOU'RE NEVER
TOO OLD TO...

... INVENT A
NEW COCKTAIL.

YOU'RE NEVER
TOO OLD TO...

... GO BACKPACKING.

YOU'RE NEVER
TOO OLD TO...

... HAVE CHAMPAGNE
FOR BREAKFAST.

WHY DID WE WAIT FOR ANY
THING? - WHY NOT SEIZE
THE PLEASURE AT ONCE?

Jane Austen

YOU'RE NEVER
TOO OLD TO...

... DREAM ABOUT BEING
ABLE TO FLY.

YOU'RE NEVER
TOO OLD TO...

... WEAR A COSTUME.

DO ANYTHING,
BUT LET IT
PRODUCE JOY.

Henry Miller

YOU'RE NEVER
TOO OLD TO...

... HAVE WHIPPED CREAM
AND SPRINKLES.

YOU'RE NEVER
TOO OLD TO...

... HAVE A BEAUTIFUL MAN
OR WOMAN ON EACH ARM.

YOU'RE NEVER
TOO OLD TO...

... GO BACK TO SCHOOL.

YOU'RE NEVER
TOO OLD TO...

... STAY UP LATE WATCHING
HORROR MOVIES.

HAPPINESS, NOT IN
ANOTHER PLACE BUT
THIS PLACE... NOT
FOR ANOTHER HOUR,
BUT THIS HOUR.

Walt Whitman

YOU'RE NEVER
TOO OLD TO...

... HAVE A
SPRING CLEAN.

YOU'RE NEVER
TOO OLD TO...

... HAVE A SECOND DINNER.

YOU'RE NEVER
TOO OLD TO...

... TELL A STRANGER THAT
THEY LOOK FANTASTIC.

YOU'RE NEVER
TOO OLD TO...

... TURN UP THE MUSIC.

WHAT IS DONE
IN LOVE IS
DONE WELL.

Vincent Van Gogh

YOU'RE NEVER
TOO OLD TO...

... FALL BRIEFLY IN LOVE
WITH YOUR WAITER OR
WAITRESS.

YOU'RE NEVER
TOO OLD TO...

... START A CONGA LINE.

LIFE ISN'T ABOUT FINDING YOURSELF. LIFE IS ABOUT CREATING YOURSELF.

George Bernard Shaw

YOU'RE NEVER
TOO OLD TO...

... SLIP INTO SOMETHING
"MORE COMFORTABLE".

WAIT NOT TILL
TOMORROW; GATHER
THE ROSES OF
LIFE TODAY.

Pierre de Ronsard

YOU'RE NEVER
TOO OLD TO...

... SIT AT THE FRONT OF
THE ROLLER COASTER.

YOU'RE NEVER
TOO OLD TO...

... PERFECT THE ART OF
TOASTING MARSHMALLOWS
ON A CAMPFIRE.

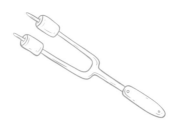

IF NOT ME, WHO?
IF NOT NOW, WHEN?

Hillel the Elder

YOU'RE NEVER
TOO OLD TO...

... ENJOY PARIS
IN SPRINGTIME.

YOU'RE NEVER
TOO OLD TO...

... MAKE IT
A DOUBLE.

YOU'RE NEVER
TOO OLD TO...

... ORDER IT SHAKEN,
NOT STIRRED.

YOU'RE NEVER
TOO OLD TO...

... ASK SOMEONE
TO DANCE.

YOU'RE NEVER
TOO OLD TO...

... BE KING
OR QUEEN OF
THE BBQ.

YOU'RE NEVER
TOO OLD TO...

... BE AT THE FRONT OF THE
SHOW, EVEN IF IT'S IN A
CONCERT HALL, NOT
A STADIUM.

LIFE IS EITHER
A DARING ADVENTURE
OR NOTHING.

Helen Keller

YOU'RE NEVER
TOO OLD TO...

... HAVE A STICK-ON
MOUSTACHE FOR EVERY DAY
OF THE WEEK. MONDAY IS
THE "SELLECK".

YOU'RE NEVER
TOO OLD TO...

... INVENT THE ULTIMATE
SANDWICH. THE "ONE OF
EACH", ANYONE?

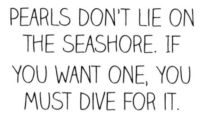

YOU'RE NEVER
TOO OLD TO...

... BEAT YOUR
PERSONAL BEST.

YOU'RE NEVER
TOO OLD TO...

... GET BUTTERFLIES IN
YOUR STOMACH.

YOU'RE NEVER
TOO OLD TO...

... BE SOMEONE'S HERO.

YOU'RE NEVER
TOO OLD TO...

... MAKE YOUR DREAMS
COME TRUE.

THE ONLY REASON
TO BE ALIVE IS
TO ENJOY IT.

Rita Mae Brown

If you're interested in finding out more about our books, find us on Facebook at **Summersdale Publishers** and follow us on Twitter at **@Summersdale**.

www.summersdale.com

Image Credits

p.1 © NotionPic/Shutterstock.com, p.7 © Curly Pat/Shutterstock.com, pp.8, 21, 32, 45, 56, 69, 80, 93, 106, 117, 130, 141, 154 © Rudenko Roman/Shutterstock.com & © Astarina/Shutterstock.com, p.9 © hchjjl/Shutterstock.com, pp.10, 18, 79, 94, 115, 120, 128 © Daniela Barreto/Shutterstock.com, pp.12, 89, 134 © Visual Generation/Shutterstock.com, p.15, 140 © Gabrielng/Shutterstock.com, p.17 © Alexander_P/Shutterstock.com, p.20 © TonTonic/Shutterstock.com, pp.22, 84, 155 © mhatzapa/Shutterstock.com, p.25 © Azulzl/Shutterstock.com, p.26 © LAATA9/Shutterstock.com, p.28 © Poltorak/Shutterstock.com, p.30 © Nataliia Machula/Shutterstock.com, p.33 © Anysh/Shutterstock.com, p.34 © Macrovector/Shutterstock.com, pp.36, 57, 70, 73 © LHF Graphics/Shutterstock.com, p.38 © AVA Bitter/Shutterstock.com, pp.41, 63, 83 © advent/Shutterstock.com, p.43 © Squirrell/Shutterstock.com, pp.44, 92, 123 © Vector Tradition/Shutterstock.com, p.46 © alicedaniel/Shutterstock.com, p.49 © Vik Y/Shutterstock.com, p.51 © il67/Shutterstock.com, p.52 © AlexHliv/Shutterstock.com, p.55 © handini_atmodiwiryo/Shutterstock.com, p.59 © Uncle Leo/Shutterstock.com, p.60 © Marek Trawczynski/Shutterstock.com, p.65 © Mureu/Shutterstock.com, p.66 © Vectorcarrot/Shutterstock.com, p.68 © Epine/Shutterstock.com, p.74 © Alfmaler/Shutterstock.com, p.76 © V_ctoria/Shutterstock.com, p.81 © Afanasia/Shutterstock.com, pp.87, 147 © pimlena/Shutterstock.com, p.90 © MoreVector/Shutterstock.com, p.97 © Aleks Melnik/Shutterstock.com, p.99 © ArtMari/Shutterstock.com, p.100 © Danussa/Shutterstock.com, p.103 © Fotonium/Shutterstock.com, p.104 © Janos Levente/Shutterstock.com, p.107 © shtiel/Shutterstock.com, p.108 © sabbracadabra/Shutterstock.com, pp.110, 111, 131 © Kamieshkova/Shutterstock.com, p.112 © Frolova Polina/Shutterstock.com, p.116 © nikiteev_konstantin/Shutterstock.com, p.119 © Pinchuk Oleksandra/Shutterstock.com, pp.124, 143 © Padma Sanjaya/Shutterstock.com, p.126 © AuraArt/Shutterstock.com, p.132 © Cat_arch_angel/Shutterstock.com, p.137 © Maria Ticce/Shutterstock.com, p.139 © kates_illustrations/Shutterstock.com, p.145 © artnLera/Shutterstock.com, p.149 © La puma/Shutterstock.com, p.150 © Fafarumba/Shutterstock.com, p.152 © makeitdouble/Shutterstock.com, p.156 © Gil C/Shutterstock.com, p.158 © Murvin/Shutterstock.com